find out about minibeasts

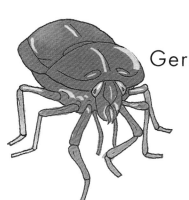

Written and edited by
Gerald Legg and Kay Barnham

Designed by
Chris Leishman

Illustrated by
Rachael O'Neill

Contents

Chrysalis Children's Books

All about minibeasts

Most of the animals in the world are **minibeasts**. These tiny creatures creep, crawl, fly and wriggle around everywhere.

Spiders and **scorpions** have eight legs.

Slugs and **snails** slither along the ground.

Centipedes run about on lots of legs.

Three-quarters of all the animals in the world are insects.

Butterflies flap their wings to fly.

Slower-moving **millipedes** have many legs too.

Insects have six legs and their bodies are divided into three parts.

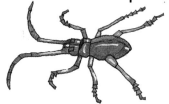

Molluscs have soft bodies but no legs. They include slugs and snails.

Arachnids are eight-legged. Their bodies are in two parts.

3

Soft bodies

Soft-bodied minibeasts live in dark, damp places. They squeeze through soil and compost, looking for food.

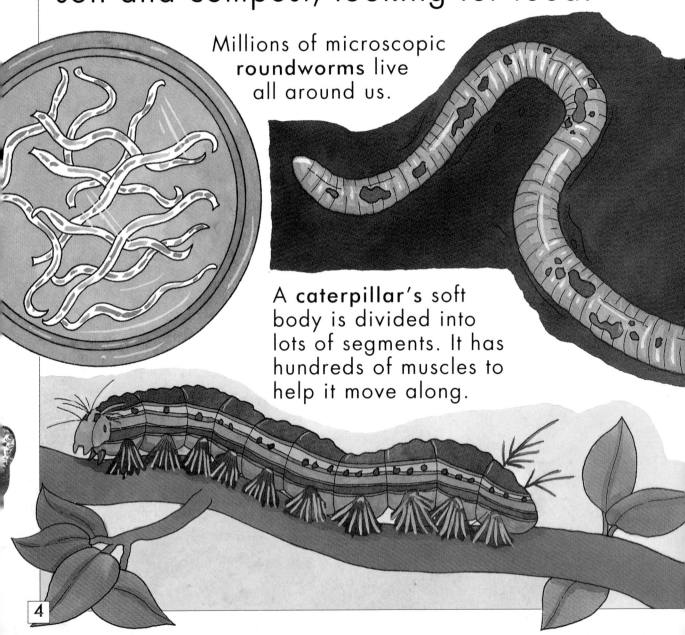

Millions of microscopic **roundworms** live all around us.

A **caterpillar's** soft body is divided into lots of segments. It has hundreds of muscles to help it move along.

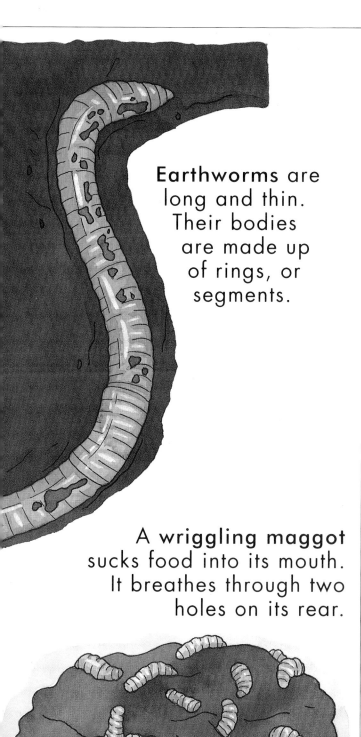

Earthworms are long and thin. Their bodies are made up of rings, or segments.

A **wriggling maggot** sucks food into its mouth. It breathes through two holes on its rear.

Leeches have soft bodies. Most of them live in water.

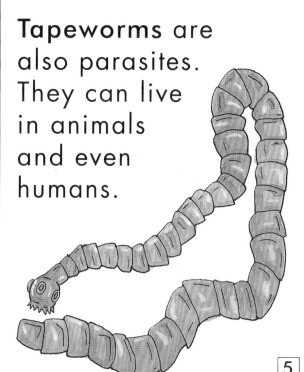

Most leeches live on other animals. Creatures that do this are called **parasites**.

Tapeworms are also parasites. They can live in animals and even humans.

Snails, slugs and shells

A shell protects the snail inside and stops its body from drying up. Slugs are like snails, but do not have shells.

Shells can be all sorts of colours and sizes.

Snails go inside their shells to sleep.

The largest snail ever found was a Giant African snail. It weighed almost as much as a kilogram bag of sugar.

Many slugs eat plants and cause a lot of damage.

Snails and slugs slide along the ground on a special **foot**. They slither along on a layer of slime.

Slugs and snails have special **tongues** covered in tiny teeth. They use their tongues to nibble at food.

Wings

Most insects fly around to find food and escape from enemies. Different insects need different kinds of wings.

Dragonflies have very delicate wings with lots of tiny veins running through them. They swoop down and catch other insects for food.

Ladybird beetle

A beetle's tough front wings protect its delicate flying wings underneath.

The tiny **fairy fly** and **plume moth** have feathery wings.

Fairy fly

Plume moth

Butterflies and **moths** have four wings. These are covered in tiny coloured scales, which form a pattern.

Most insects have four wings. The best flyers are **flies**, which have two wings.

Flies used to have four wings. Now they have tiny stumps where their second set used to be.

Suits of armour

Insects, spiders, woodlice and mites have their skeletons on the outside. This protects the soft body underneath.

The bodies of these minibeasts are divided into segments. There are joints in between so that their bodies can bend and move.

Spider

Segment

Joint

Grasshoppers make noises by rubbing their wings and legs together.

The heaviest insect in the world is the Goliath beetle. It can weigh up to 100 grams.

Mites are some of the tiniest minibeasts with armour.

When one kind of **woodlouse** is in danger, it rolls up into a ball to protect itself.

Shield bugs have hard, shield-shaped backs.

As the minibeast grows, the hard outer skeleton stays the same size.

The skeleton cracks and falls off, to show a new soft skeleton beneath.

The minibeast puffs up the new skeleton before it hardens. This gives it room to grow later.

Baby minibeasts

Most minibeasts hatch from eggs. When they are born, some young minibeasts look like smaller versions of adults.

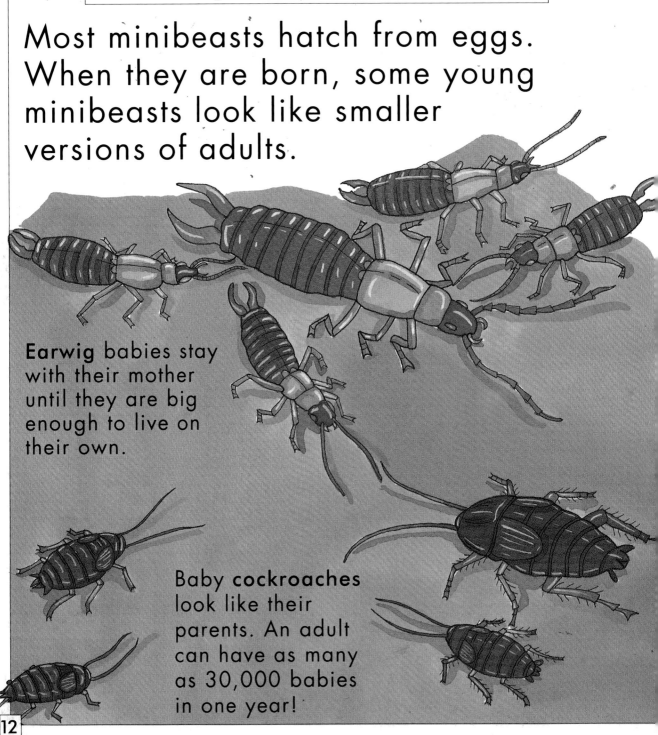

Earwig babies stay with their mother until they are big enough to live on their own.

Baby **cockroaches** look like their parents. An adult can have as many as 30,000 babies in one year!

Baby locusts are called **hoppers**. Swarms of locust hoppers eat everything in their path as they move along.

Baby **scorpions** can use their sting to catch food, just like adult scorpions.

Young **woodlice** look just like their parents but they are a paler colour.

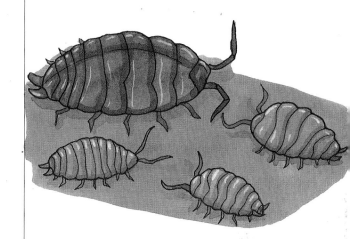

A baby **snail's** shell is smaller and less coiled than an adult's shell.

Changing

When minibeasts, such as flies, beetles and butterflies hatch, they look nothing like the adults that they will change into. These young minibeasts are called larvae.

Caterpillar

Butterflies lay eggs, which hatch into larvae. These larvae are called caterpillars.

A larva then changes into a chrysalis.

Butterfly chrysalis

14

Adult peacock butterfly

The larva changes inside the chrysalis and hatches as an adult.

Ladybird larvae feed on aphids.

Stag beetle larvae live in logs for years, before they tunnel out as adults.

Black fly larvae live in streams and ponds.

15

Living together

Most minibeasts lay their eggs and leave their young to hatch and grow up alone. The others look after their young.

Baby **scorpions** ride on their mothers' backs.

Young **woodlice** cling to their mothers until they are old enough to look after themselves.

Bees live together in a hive. The queen bee is the only female who lays any eggs. Males breed and the female workers look after the young bees.

A queen termite can lay nearly 50,000 eggs a day and she may live for 25 years!

Paper wasps house their young in nests made of paper.

A mother **spider** sometimes feeds her spiderlings with food from her mouth.

Termite homes are called mounds. Some termite mounds can be as tall as 9 metres.

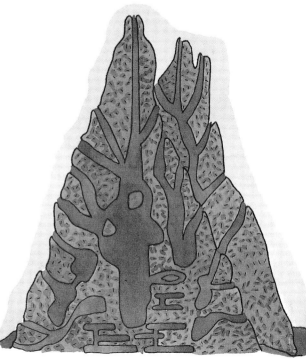

They are full of tiny tunnels leading to the surface, so there is always a supply of fresh air.

17

Eating

Minibeasts can bite or chew with their jaws. Some have mouthparts like a small hollow needle, for sucking blood or plant juices.

A **mosquito's** sharp jaws cut a hole in skin. It sucks up blood through a long tube.

Fleas can jump half a metre to reach their prey.

Ticks stick their jaws into skin. Their bodies swell as they suck up blood.

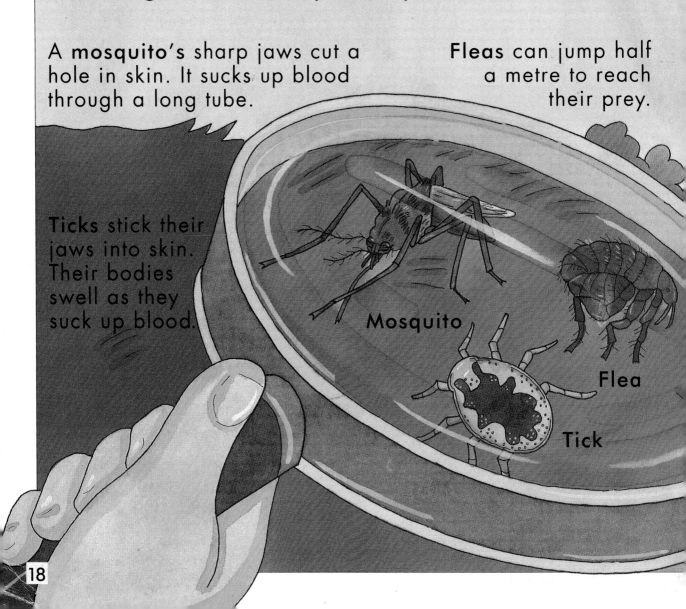

Mosquito

Flea

Tick

Thousands of tiny **aphids** feed on plant juices.

Houseflies have a special way of eating. First they vomit on food to soften it. Then they suck both the food and vomit up their sucking tube.

Some **moths** have very long tongues. They can reach deep down into a flower to feed on the sweet nectar.

Hunting

Some minibeasts hunt other creatures for food. They have strong jaws and some use poison to paralyse or kill their prey.

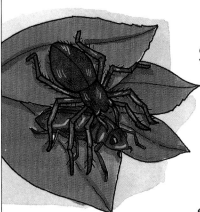

Spiders have jaws which inject their victims with poison.

Net-throwing spiders throw nets on top of their prey.

Wasps sting their prey to paralyse them. The victims are then fed to wasp larvae.

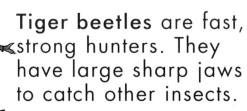

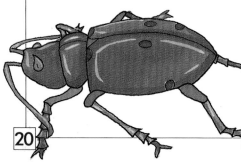

Tiger beetles are fast, strong hunters. They have large sharp jaws to catch other insects.

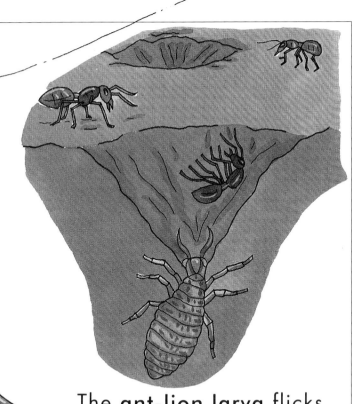

A **spider** uses its web to catch flying insects. The web is made of sticky silk.

The **ant-lion larva** flicks sand at passing insects from the bottom of its hole. They fall down into its waiting jaws.

Tiny **false scorpions** live among soil and dead leaves. They catch springtails and mites there.

Fun Fact

Black-widow spiders are the most deadly spiders in the world.

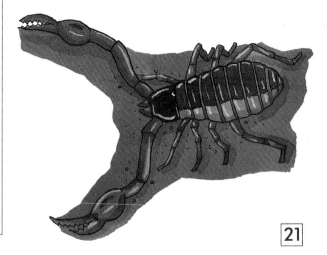

21

Hiding and scaring

Minibeasts are often coloured to match their surroundings. This helps them to hide from hunters or surprise their prey.

Praying mantids are the same colour as the plant they sit on.

When a **butterfly** lands, it becomes the mantid's meal.

Thornbugs look just like thorns so that larger creatures will not attack them while they drink plant juices.

A **leaf shoemaker butterfly** looks exactly like a rotting leaf!

Some minibeasts are brightly coloured to scare other creatures away.

The **emperor moth** has false eyes on its wings. It pretends to be dangerous, but is quite harmless.

The **five-spot burnet moth** has colourful wings to warn others that it is poisonous to eat.

23

Index

Edited by Kay Barnham
Managing Editor: Nicola Wright
Design Manager: Kate Buxton
Production: Zoë Fawcett
Printed in China

ISBN 1 84238 659 6

10 9 8 7 6 5 4 3 2 1

This edition first published in 2003 by
Chrysalis Children's Books
The Chrysalis Building, Bramley Rd, London W10 6SP

Copyright © Chrysalis Books PLC